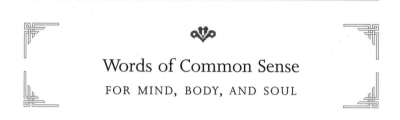

Words of Common Sense

FOR MIND, BODY, AND SOUL

One pound of learning requires
ten pounds of common sense
to apply it.
—PERSIAN

Common sense is not common.
—SIR JOHN TEMPLETON

Words of Common Sense

FOR MIND, BODY, AND SOUL

Brother David Steindl-Rast
Foreword by Thomas Moore

Templeton Foundation Press
Philadelphia & London

Templeton Foundation Press
Five Radnor Corporate Center, Suite 120
100 Matsonford Road
Radnor, Pennsylvania 19087
www.templetonpress.org

Library of Congress Cataloging-in-Publication Data
Steindl-Rast, David.
Words of common sense for mind, body, and soul /
David Steindl-Rast.
p. cm.
ISBN 1-890151-98-X (cloth : alk. paper)
1. Common sense. 2. Conduct of life.
3. Jesus Christ—Parables.
4. Proverbs—History and criticism.   I. Title.
BJ1595.S764 2002
170'.44—dc21   2002009187

Designed and typeset by Joanna Hill and Helene Krasney
Printed by Versa Press, Inc.
Printed in the United States of America
02 03 04 05 06   10 9 8 7 6 5 4 3 2 1

Dedicated to the webteam of

www.gratefulness.org

because gratitude is the

finest flower of Common Sense.

Contents

Acknowledgments

As an author, I am keenly aware that it takes the common effort of many people to bring about a book. This book owes much to the kindness and efficiency of Joanna Hill, Laura Barrett, and their coworkers at the Templeton Press; and to Thomas Moore's gracious and thought-provoking introduction. My thanks go also to Candice Fuhrman, my charming and competent agent; to Patricia Campbell Carlson for her personal assistance in every phase of preparing the manuscript; to Rosemarie Primault for generous research and advice; to Daniel Uvanovic for helping me clarify the concept of common sense; and to all the friends who offered helpful comments on early drafts. I owe a great debt to John Dominic Crossan, whose books In Parables and Cliffs of Fall gave me a new perspective on the parables of Jesus; and to

Selwyn Gurney Champion, M.D., for his classic collection of proverbs from all parts of the world. Above all, I am grateful to the countless people throughout the ages—from beggars to queens—who passed on to us through proverbs the wisdom of common sense. Last not least, my thanks to Gumpa, my helper who showed considerable common sense as message-carrying cat.

Introduction

BY THOMAS MOORE

It's been a long time since I have read anything so fresh, so useful, and so full of common sense as these thoughts of Brother David. Many write about wisdom as if it were a prize to be gained after many decades of study and meditation, but common sense is immediate. You can be young or old, practical or dreamy, schooled or the salt of the earth and enjoy common sense. Brother David writes for you and for me, for anyone who wants to live a life that is rich in significance and pleasure. He gives common sense its depth, going far beyond any anti-intellectual or vulgar sense of the term.

Something in modern life makes us anything but common. Its two special forms of neurosis are narcissism and depression. The first comes about because we find it difficult to be individuals in a world that treats us as parts of a great social machine, not as unique members of a community. The second appears frequently because, for all the convenience and entertainment available through modern achievement, generally we no longer have the sheer joy of being alive and connected to the natural world and to each other. Both are symptoms of a loss of commonality.

Narcissism is the awkward and ineffective attempt to be somebody. We have to insist on our mere presence: "Look what I can do! I'm special, chosen, on the right side of things, and you're not!" The narcissist thinks he knows how everyone else should think and live—like him. But a person of common sense enjoys sharing wisdom with everyone else. He can learn from his neighbor, just as he can make a contribution.

Naturally, as in most common sense matters, there is a paradox at work: The only way to feel like somebody is to be an active member of community. The narcissist can't surrender to the common. She daydreams of being exceptional and remarkably successful. But a person comfortable with herself can be at home with others. He senses the beauty and sufficiency in being a member of the human race and a being among other beings of nature. She enjoys the existence and achievement of someone else. He wants species to survive and dreams of lying down with the lamb and the wolf. Over many years of doing psychotherapy, I have heard many dreams in which the dreamer without a thought beats and kills animals just because they are there. With a little common sense, we could live in harmony with nature.

A related malady is the cult of celebrity. Ordinary people show signs of near insane mania in the presence of fame. Those who are famous tell of the loneliness they sometimes feel at being segregated from the common, but they also feel fulfilled and complete at having extricated themselves. Many who will never be famous feel condemned to ordinariness, and they can only dream impossibly of their escape from the herd.

I think we can find relief from both the hunger for individuality and the sadness of the collective by overcoming the split between the extraordinary life and life in community. But this has to be done concretely. Lonely men or women, desperate for love and longing for an identity, could discover the treasure they seek through service and engagement. For another paradox rules: you find the precious self by surrendering your self. Your soul is not to be found in the empty halls of your own personality but in the needy and confused lives of neighbors— the children in need and the adults trying to get along. The best way to make sense of your life is to contribute to the life of someone else.

Common sense is a sense of the common, the awareness that we discover who and what we are in relationship, not only to people but also to everything that is. That is why I love the many sparkling proverbs Brother David has collected: They tell in colloquial, witty, and imaginative ways what happens to us all on ordinary days and in our ordinary lives. They are not rules for any select individual but apply to everyone. Call them archetypal or mythic. They place us in touch with our humanity and offer a foundation for thinking freshly about everyday situations.

Connecting these proverbs to the parables of Jesus helps me appreciate the role of religion in the common life. Religious groups suffer the neurosis of modernism just as individuals do. They have to compete and insist on their special claims to truth. They often forget common sense and even go against it in a feverish and desperate effort to be special. But there is nothing more common than the spiritual life and the rich imagination of the religions. Each tradition speaks to every man, woman, and child on earth. The difference in expression is only the richness of the imagination in which common sense finds power and persuasiveness.

Another paradox: The more particular the expression, the more it applies to everyone. I don't try to make all the religions sound alike. In their differences lies their commonality. Esperanto of the spiritual life, an artificially extricated language of virtue and wisdom, would be a caricature of common sense. Noting common concerns and lessons among Jesus, Mohammed, and the Buddha brings to light a certain beauty and persuasiveness, but so do all the precious differences and unique ways and teachings. Common sense is not an intellectual meatball, a ground round of rich intellectual nurturance made into a bland patty of truisms. Common sense is a sharp, resonant realization of how things are in the present circumstance and across the globe.

In a world grown small through communications and travel especially, we need a common sense approach to conflicts and problems. Leaders and politicians tend to make it all too complicated, so that we never advance toward a positive and lasting peace. The issues are really quite simple: We want life in abundance. We want our children to be safe, healthy, and happy. We are mice of the same hole. One hand washes another. Every cabin has its mosquito, but a single bracelet doesn't jingle.

Common sense, and only common sense as defined by Brother David, could get us out of our racial, gender, and sexual conflicts. It could resolve the problems of world poverty and hunger, but apparently, we don't have the common sense to use it. The choice of uncommon sense—complicated solutions to dire problems—merely temporizes. It serves as a defense against the most apparent solutions that threaten the status quo, which in turn depends on inequality. We avoid common sense precisely because it would lead to the necessary changes.

Rarely am I so pleased with a book and feel its raw power. Brother David has not written this overnight. He has brought a lifetime of reflection and experience to a theme that has infinitely more importance and practicality than it appears to have. He has by-passed the more familiar route of artificial complexity, finding his way instead through the more common way that is more subtle and profound. He describes a way to think and feel with our fellow beings and discover solutions to our problems that are deeply in tune with our humanity. ✸

Words of Common Sense

FOR MIND, BODY, AND SOUL

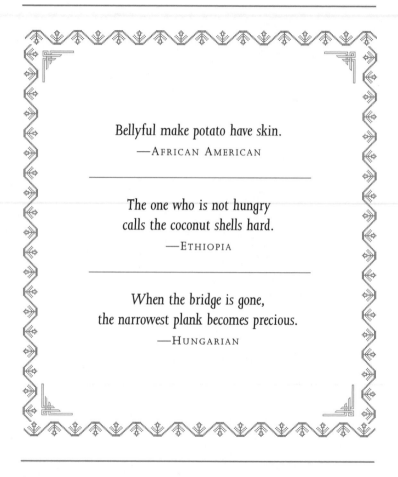

Bellyful make potato have skin.
—AFRICAN AMERICAN

The one who is not hungry
calls the coconut shells hard.
—ETHIOPIA

When the bridge is gone,
the narrowest plank becomes precious.
—HUNGARIAN

What Is Common Sense?

You have heard the old saying, "Common sense is anything but common," and there is some truth to it. We don't have to look far to find ample proof: Much of what is said and done in our world is certainly not based on common sense. Yet, how do we become aware of this—except by using the common sense we have? We do have it; we just fail to follow it. The language we use shows that we know this. A friend may grab you by the shoulders and exclaim in exasperation, "For heaven's sake, use common sense!" Doesn't this imply that you'd have all the common sense you needed, if only you would use it? What is uncommon is not common sense, but willingness to live by it.

Why is this so? What is our problem? Well, when we talk about using common sense it sounds as if we need only apply

Never depend too much
on the blackberry blossoms.

—AFRICAN AMERICAN

Don't bet on a tater hill
before the grabblin' time.

—AFRICAN AMERICAN

Not every dark cloud brings rain.

—HAYA, EAST AFRICA

Don't count your chickens
before they hatch.

—ENGLISH

our mind to it the way we apply a wrench to a leaking pipe; this puts us on the wrong track. Truly to have common sense means no less than living by it, breathing it as we breathe the air shared by all living beings. We must sense what is common before we can think common-sense thoughts. Can we expect common sense to get into our heads unless we open our hearts, breathe deeply, and get a sense of what we all have in common?

To witness life-in-common you need only look at some little stretch of hedgerow or woods: how the trees share their bark with mosses and lichens; how the bushes, herbs, and flowers interact with one another; what a complex give-and-take connects them with the soil, its mulch, minerals, and micro-organisms—with insects, spiders, worms, and other creeping creatures, with birds and animals, with wind and rain and sunlight and mist. A vibrant common sense animates the whole.

Let's not make this image too romantic, though. The harmony we find in nature is different from our wishful thinking; the lion is not about to lie down with the lamb—not even the robin with the earthworm, or the cat with the robin. "Food chain" is too antiseptic; it makes us forget the stark facts: living creatures live by killing and eating each other. Nature is one big eat-and-be-eaten. But why not call it a banquet—a wedding banquet, if you will. While creatures feast on others, they mate with their own kind. Every single flower in the meadow is a lavish display of innocent sex in its naked glory—before a cow eats it up. The hum and buzz of it all is the music of one great wedding feast. A common harmony guides the steps of each creature in this fierce but joyful dance of all with all.

All, except us humans. We are the only awkward ones, the wallflowers at this dance. We are unique in nature, and this is a great gift, but it becomes our downfall. We tend to confuse the truth that we are different with the illusion of being separate. This dulls our sense of the common rhythm and makes us fall out of step in the great dance.

Simple people have less of a problem here. I am not referring to simpletons; someone like His Holiness the Dalai Lama provides an example of genuine simplicity that is quite compatible with a high degree of sophistication. What gets in the way of simplicity is not sophistication but self-importance, with all the complications it creates. The more lightly we take ourselves, the more we leave the narrow confines of our little egos behind and enter the wide-open spaces of our true selves. Men and women who expand themselves in this way find common ground and great inner freedom. Rid of pretense, they seem to breathe more easily. They radiate a sense of being at home in the universe and everybody feels at home with them. They speak a universal language; anyone can understand them. A Swiss proverb even claims, "If you have common sense, you can talk to cattle."

It is a gift to meet people who are fluent in the language of common sense. I remember one of them from my childhood: our hunchback neighbor, Frau Schliffsteiner. She certainly could talk to cattle; she could talk to goats and dogs and cats, to pigeons and sparrows, to toads and to the potted geranium plants on her windowsill, to the seedlings in her garden bed. Above all, she could talk to people of any kind—from the village bum to the schoolmaster of our two-room school (and he

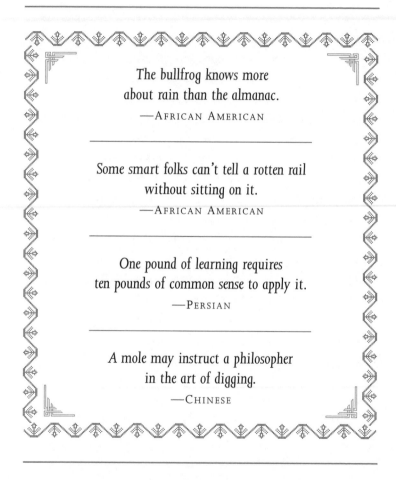

The bullfrog knows more
about rain than the almanac.

—AFRICAN AMERICAN

Some smart folks can't tell a rotten rail
without sitting on it.

—AFRICAN AMERICAN

One pound of learning requires
ten pounds of common sense to apply it.

—PERSIAN

A mole may instruct a philosopher
in the art of digging.

—CHINESE

was far above everyone; he could even play the piano). In her simplicity, she treated all people as family members, and her family quite naturally included the animals and plants. She seemed to know their secrets. She knew which herbs made the right tea against a bellyache and which leaves made your finger heal quickly when you had cut yourself. In olden times, they might have called her a witch, but surely she was a good witch—and a sensible one.

Her neighbors would sip coffee with her and talk and talk about all that weighed on their hearts and minds. They always felt lighter afterwards—and it wasn't because of her coffee; that was a sorry brew out of the few coffee beans she could afford. What she gave to those who came to her was a sense of belonging: she let them breathe the healing air of common sense. After all, healing on any level—mind, body, soul, spirit—is, as a Tamil proverb puts it, "Medicine one-fourth, common sense three-fourth."

Common sense brings about healing because it is more than a way of thinking; it is a way of living, a way of acting, a way of doing what makes sense—of doing it spontaneously, unselfconsciously, effortlessly. You experience a glimpse of this when you "hit the sweet spot" in jogging, typing, dancing, or whatever the activity may be: suddenly you are "in the flow" and everything happens smoothly in the right way and at the right moment. Now imagine being able to stay "in the flow," to maintain this attitude of self-forgetful spontaneity. Wouldn't the vigor and ease of "the sweet spot" continually keep your spirit aglow, your soul at peace, your mind alert, and your body healthy? Few may be able to attain so high a goal, but all of us can strive for it.

A lifetime may not be long enough to attune ourselves fully to the harmony of the universe. But just to become aware that we can resonate with it—that alone can be like waking up from a dream. At the dawn of Western thought, the Greek philosopher Heraclitus recognized this: "The waking have one world in common," he wrote, "sleepers have each a private world of their own. We should not act or speak as if we were asleep." The African Bantu say it with more zest in a proverb: "There are forty kinds of lunacy, but only one kind of common sense."

"Although the *Logos* is common to all, most people live as if they had each their own private intelligence," Heraclitus lamented. And he added: "We should let ourselves be guided by what is common to all." Lao Tsu used the word *Tao* for this guiding principle "that brings the people of the world into harmony of heart." We need our own term and we do have an excellent English phrase for it: *common sense*—the inner guidance we have in common with all and that alone enables us to act in ways that make sense. ✿

One hand washes the other.

—ANCIENT ROMAN

One finger can't catch fleas.

—AFRICAN AMERICAN

One hand can't tie a bundle.

—BASA

Proverbs and Common Sense

L ike slick fish, proverbs have managed to slide through the nets of scholars who set out to catch them in a definition. One thing is certain, however: A proverb is a common saying that makes eminent sense to those who use it. The natural habitat of proverbs is in the waters of common sense. They swim with equal ease in the different strata of a given society: "Whoever has a proverb is worthy of attention," the Chinese say, "be it a mandarin or a coolie." They are common to far distant geographic areas, migrating from country to country and from language to language. Not even the waterfalls that separate period from period in history can stop proverbs, and some of them have remained common throughout vastly different eras, retaining their wiggling vitality for thousands of years.

More than two thousand years ago, the Roman scholar Varro wrote, "Non omnes, qui habent citharam, sunt citharaoes" (They are not all harpists who own a harp). He may have created a proverb, or—more likely—recorded one that was already an old saw. At any rate, through Varro it became popular, and its popularity was still so strong a thousand years later that many new proverbs were created on its pattern. "They are not all hunters who blow horns." "They are not all cooks who carry long knives." And, "They are not all friends who laugh at you." The Dutch people were particularly fond of this last one ("Zijn niet alle frienden, die hem toelachen") and seemed to have brought it to the West Indies. There it survives today— another thousand years later—in an African American version: "They are not all friends who grin showing their teeth." Other proverbs have had a long life, too. Some fifteen hundred years ago, Plutarch had already quoted, "The wearer knows best where the shoe pinches." His contemporary, St. Jerome, called "Don't look a gift horse in the mouth!" an old saw. He had fished it up from the vernacular, the language of common people, the language into which he was translating the Bible.

When it comes to proverbs, I am a passionate fisherman. Since the waters of common sense flow in every part of the world, we may be lucky and catch the same proverb in streams thousands of miles apart—or rather, find the same insight turned into a proverb by an altogether different culture. In New York, they say "Every family has a skeleton in the closet." In the West Indies, it becomes "Every house have him dirty corner," and in the southern United States, "Every cabin has its mosquito." For the Haya in East Africa, it is "Every hill has its leopard," and the Jabo give a special twist to that skeleton in the closet: "Chicken says, 'If you scratch too hard, you come upon the bones of your mother.'" To find the same with a difference is always a thrill.

Even within the same culture, you may find a delightful variety of images to get the same idea across. Which of these four proverbs would you choose to tell someone "You had it coming"? "If you won't stand blow, no play with stick." "One that carries straw mustn't fool with fire." "If you lay with the puppy, you get bitten by the fleas." "One who swims with fish must eat worms." All four of them come out of African American

If fool no go market,
bad something never sell.
—AFRICAN AMERICAN

One eye is enough for the merchant,
but the buyer needs a hundred.
—BASQUE

There are more foolish buyers
than sellers.
—BELGIAN

culture with its colorful imagery. There is no better way for coming to know a given culture than to savor its oral tradition of proverbs. Unfortunately, the media tend to make language sterile and proverbs are becoming an endangered species.

In the Austria of my childhood, everyone seemed to agree with the Basque proverb "Old words: wise words," or with the English, "All good sense of the world runs into proverbs." Besides, as the Arabs know, "A proverb is to speech what salt is to food." Cicero had already spoken of "salting" his elegant Latin prose with proverbs, and my Great Aunt Jenny, who liked lots of salt on her potatoes, salted the advice she gave us children with proverbs too. The mailman, the gypsies, and the tinker who came to the door used proverbs. So did the pastor, the butcher, and above all our tutor. None of them knew that unimaginably far away, in the Sudan, the Ojai said, "For every occasion there is a proverb." But they would all have agreed that proverbs were "the wisdom of the common people." Everyone believed in the proverb of all proverbs, which was still current among us in its Latin form, "Vox populi, vox Dei" ("The voice of the people: God's voice").

Not always, however, does the voice of the people rise from the depths we all have in common. Some proverbs spring rather from provincial prejudice. Every country tends to put mocking labels on its neighbors and often does so in proverbs. One of them has even found its way into the Bible, "Cretans: always liars" (Titus 1:12). Village may taunt village in proverbs, handing on prejudice from generation to generation and perpetuating discord. There are also proverbs that taunt certain professions, say tailors for cheating—"A tailor cuts three sleeves for every gown"—or physicians for malpractice—"Only a doctor can kill you and go scot-free." Prejudice may also target physical traits or women. "Never trust a red beard." "Get near women: get near trouble." Or worse, "Women are the snares of Satan." Fortunately, these narrow-minded proverbs are vastly outnumbered by those which speak for the entire human community. Surprisingly often, proverbs do spring from that depth in which all communicate with all and with the divine source of all. Then we can truly hear in this voice of the people overtones of a divine voice.

For a long time now, I have been collecting proverbs, not only for their content, but also for sheer pleasure in their language. I pick them up with the same enjoyment with which I collect pebbles when I walk along the shore. Just as the tides smooth and polish pebbles, daily use shapes proverbs until not one excess word is left. One proverb, for instance, uses only two syllables to conjure up the image of ploughshares gathering rust while the plough lies idle in the barnyard: "Rest: rust." Pebbles I pick have other delightful qualities besides being smooth to the touch. Their polish brings out the design in the rock. Thus, many proverbs have obviously been shaped and reshaped as they went from mouth to mouth through the centuries, until language has found the perfect design. Parallelism is a favorite pattern. "Barking saves biting." "Like father, like son." Or this one from the African Ila, "Honor a child and it will honor you." Sometimes alliteration is added. "Many men, many minds." "Live and learn." Some proverbs use rhyme. "A friend in need is a friend indeed." Or the African American "Buy beef, you buy bone; buy land, you buy rock stone." In Friesland they say, "Calf love: half love; old love: cold love."

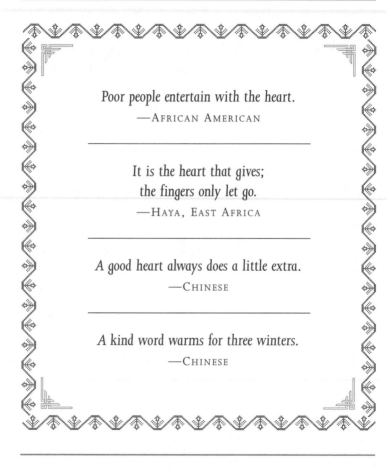

Poor people entertain with the heart.
—African American

It is the heart that gives;
the fingers only let go.
—Haya, East Africa

A good heart always does a little extra.
—Chinese

A kind word warms for three winters.
—Chinese

When the pebbles collected wet from the shore dry out, they lose their luster. Similarly, proverbs collected in books tend to be dull. It is in the living flow of speech that they sparkle. Sometimes, though, their imagery is so unmistakably part of a culture in which the flow of conversation glitters with proverbs that they seem to retain their freshness. For instance, two African American ones: "Bull old, take wis-wis [straw] tie him" and "When you go to a donkey house, don't talk about ears." African culture comes alive in proverbs like the following: "While the hyena is drinking, the dog can only watch." "One small straw suffices to suck honey from the hive." "When you have but one garment, you don't wash it on a rainy day." Here's an East African version of "Forewarned is forearmed": "The hippopotamus that shows itself doesn't upset the boat." What could be more typically Swiss than "Everything may be bought, but time"? And finally a proverb that is as Dutch as tulips or wooden shoes: "Who wants the last drop out of the can, gets the lid on the nose."

In one type of proverb, common sense reaches its perfect expression. At first sight, proverbs of this sort may appear

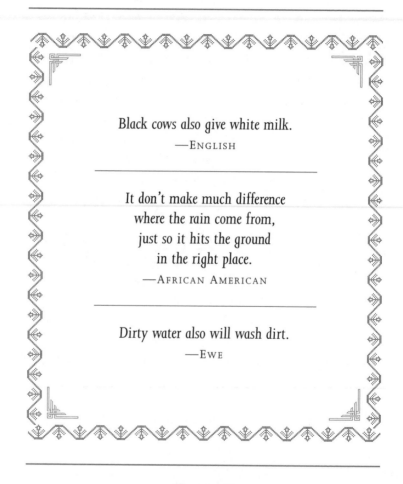

Black cows also give white milk.
—ENGLISH

It don't make much difference
where the rain come from,
just so it hits the ground
in the right place.
—AFRICAN AMERICAN

Dirty water also will wash dirt.
—EWE

homespun—like many great things. In fact, "homespun" is a good word to describe them if we give to "home" its deepest meaning. Common sense is the thinking and feeling and willing that we share with the whole Earth Household. There is our true home, and there the proverbs of this kind have been "spun." They do not philosophize or moralize; they simply hold up one image, as if to say "Look!" And the more we look, the more we see. "Under trees it rains twice" (Swiss). "A tiny needle goes through coarse cloth" (Sudan). "Dead twig shows itself when the buds come out" (African American). "Drop by drop carves the stone" (ancient Rome). These images are spun by the great Mother-of-All on the same spinning wheel on which the threads of the world itself are being spun. This is why these proverbs shine so brightly and yield ever new insights. We find images of this kind throughout the parables of Jesus. ✿

Slowly, slowly will catch the monkey.
—JABO

Drop by drop fills the pot.
—DUALA

The hindermost ox also reaches the kraal.
—DUTCH

---

*The one who runs and the one who limps
meet again at the ferry.*
—EGYPTIAN

The Common Sense Sayings of Jesus

The original message of Jesus still sparkles with freshness, and nowhere more brilliantly than in his parables. Like grains of gold in sand, these parables were deposited in the earliest layers of Christian tradition. Better than most other gospel passages, they preserve the live words of the Teacher. That Jesus taught in parables is one of the few historical facts about him that we know with certainty. Mark, the earliest gospel writer, even claims, "Without a parable he did not speak to them" (4:34). Though Mark may be overstating his case, the fact remains that we can find the essence of Jesus' message in his parables. This is true in a double sense—with regard to content and with regard to form. Parables contain the gist of what Jesus taught and his choice of the parable form is in itself an essential aspect of his message.

Mountains don't need mountains,
but humans need humans.
—BASQUE

Frost destroys only the solitary blades of grass.
—CHINESE

The third strand makes the cable.
—DUTCH

A single stick smokes but doesn't burn.
—GALLA

Sticks in a bundle cannot be broken.
—BONDEI

Many parables of Jesus resemble those proverbs in which a vivid image sparks a common-sense insight. Sometimes expanding the image into a brief narrative, Jesus pushes the inner mechanism of that type of proverb just a little further. Typically, his parables have three steps. Step one confronts us with a question: "Who of you . . . ?" (Who of you doesn't know that figs don't grow on thistles? That blind guides are not particularly reliable? That a tiny seed grows into a tall tree?) Step two is our reply. Without hesitation we answer: "Well, everybody knows this. Common sense tells us so!" But then comes step three—another question, and often a merely implicit one: "Ah, if you know it so well, why don't you act accordingly?" Laughter is the proper response. The joke is on us. We can all laugh together at the fact that we have all the common sense we need yet when it comes to the most important matters, we live like nitwits. Parable after parable is a variation on this joke.

A closer look will show us, however, that few of the parables in the gospels still work as jokes. The reason is obvious. How often can you tell the same joke to the same audience?

After a few times even the most patient ones will boo. And yet, the images Jesus used remain precious to his followers. So tradition retains and repeats the images, but turns the jokes into moralizing stories. The so-called Parable of the Good Samaritan (Luke 10:29–37) is a good example of this tendency.

The context in Luke's gospel is a discussion about loving one's neighbor. "But who is my neighbor?" someone asks. Jesus picks up the implication, "God forbid that I should be kind to someone who isn't—in the full technical sense—my neighbor!" He seems to chuckle as he answers by telling a story: "A man went down from Jerusalem to Jericho. . . . " Now remember: this man is you. The first person mentioned is often the one with whom you must identify for a joke to work. So you travel down that road, notorious for its robbers, and sure enough, one of them holds you up, beats you, strips you, and lets you lie there half dead. You are only half dead; this is important, because you must be just alive enough to see what happens next. This story is told from the perspective of the one who was mugged, and that is you.

So you lie there by the roadside and someone comes down the same road. "Oh, here comes my neighbor," your heart cries out. "He must help me!" Notice that you suddenly know who is your neighbor, now that you are in trouble. You know it, but he doesn't—or doesn't want to know; he walks right by. But wait, you get another chance. Another traveler is coming by. "Surely this one will know that he is my neighbor and will help me!" You don't know who it is, but common sense tells you that he is your neighbor. Unfortunately, he too walks by on the other side of the road. But don't give up yet (there is always a third one in a joke of this kind). Each time you hope more fervently that the stranger will know he is your neighbor. Finally a third one comes by—a Samaritan. By now the story has maneuvered you into a position where you are more than glad to welcome absolutely anyone as a neighbor. Anyone without restriction? Yes, even a Samaritan! For a Jew to think of a Samaritan as neighbor was outrageous. But here common sense suddenly clashes with public opinion and wins.

Tongue in cheek, Jesus asks, "Now which of the three, do you think, was neighbor to him who fell among the robbers?"

Who gives to me teaches me to give.
—DUTCH

---

*To give to the needy
is not to give but to sow.*
—BASQUE

---

*A gift goes out on a donkey
and comes back on a camel.*
—EGYPTIAN

The one who had asked "Who is my neighbor?" can no longer claim that he doesn't know the answer. Still, he will only say, "The one who showed him mercy." The S-word sticks in his throat; he cannot get it over his lips that a "dirty Samaritan" was indeed his neighbor.

The stories Jesus tells are not edifying tales, but jokes of this kind: You want to know who is your neighbor? Wait 'til you get into trouble. Why does your common sense work so well when you are in need? Why is your sense of our common humanity so restricted when another needs your help?

You notice the three elements typical of Jesus' parables. A strong image: yourself as victim of a mugging; a common-sense insight: when you are in need, you know that everyone is your neighbor; and the point of the joke: if you know this so well, Dummy, why act as if you didn't?

By replacing "Samaritan" with the name of a current ethnic scapegoat we, too, might get the point and laugh at our own prejudices. Of course, by calling this the Parable of the Good Samaritan, we kill the joke. Among those to whom Jesus first told the parable, the only "good Samaritan" was a dead

The horse must graze where it is tethered.

—BELGIAN

Bloom where you are planted.

—ENGLISH

The paddle you find in the canoe
is the one which will take you across.

—LIBERIA

Samaritan. Miss this point, and all that's left is an edifying tale told by a detached reporter. But when we look at the events through the eyes of the prejudiced victim with whom we identify, we are suddenly confronted with the authority of common sense. ✿

Water never loses its way.
—BANTU

Water makes its own channel.
—CHINESE

Every river run to its mamma.
—AFRICAN AMERICAN

Common Sense as Ultimate Authority

The authority to which Jesus appeals is the authority of Common Sense—with capitals, because we mean by it Divine Wisdom–Sophia—which Lao Tsu called *Tao* and Heraclitus called *Logos*. In fact, when Mark says, "In many parables Jesus spoke to them the word" (4:33), he uses for "word" the term *Logos*, which, ever since Heraclitus, carries in Greek the special meaning that we are giving to Common Sense. We must stress this point: Jesus does not appeal to divine authority enshrined in sacred Scripture, as did the priests and scribes who said, "Thus it is written. . . ." Nor does he appeal to divine authority as speaking through him, as did the prophets, who said, "Thus speaketh the Lord. . . ." When he challenges them with "Who of you . . . doesn't know this already?" Jesus appeals to the divine authority in the hearts of his hearers.

It's when you cross the ford
that your leg problems show up.
—EGYPTIAN

The dust speck always heads for the single eye.
—CHUANA

All the flies will alight on the sick goat.
—AUSTRIA

It's the sore toe that gets stubbed.
—KENYA

The neighbor will call on the day you do your hair.
—CATALONIAN

Priests, scribes, and prophets talk down at the people from the high ground of divine authority; Jesus stands on common ground with them and makes them stand on their own feet by recognizing that divine authority speaks through common sense. The implications are staggering.

Common Sense is the ultimate authority. Deep down we all know this. If the teachings of ministers and theologians can't stand up to Common Sense they crumble. If the exhortations of preachers fall short of Common Sense, they fail. When a teacher awakens us to use Common Sense ourselves, we respond as Jesus' hearers did. "They were astonished at his teaching, for he taught them as one who had authority . . ." (Mark 1:22). Mark adds, "not like the scribes"—not like the authoritarians. This comparison contains a death sentence for Jesus. Nothing is more threatening to an authoritarian mind than an appeal to the authority of Common Sense. Religious and political authoritarians alike will not rest until anyone who mobilizes Common Sense among the common people is wiped out. This is why Jesus had to die.

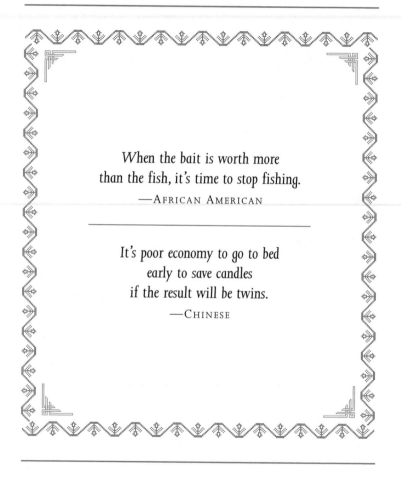

*When the bait is worth more
than the fish, it's time to stop fishing.*
—AFRICAN AMERICAN

*It's poor economy to go to bed
early to save candles
if the result will be twins.*
—CHINESE

Authority as such is of course a good thing. It is by definition a firm foundation for knowing and acting. A community will elevate those who excel in leadership skills and wise counsel to positions of authority and entrust them with power. But power corrupts. Inevitably, some who do not possess the necessary qualifications will acquire positions of authority and hold on to them. They will wield power without the required wisdom and compassion. Such authoritarians are the sworn enemies of genuine authority grounded in Common Sense. They will try to maintain their hollow power through spreading fear. Fear keeps Common Sense down—fear of losing your job if you speak up and question policies that go against common sense; fear of being ostracized if you question authority.

Refusal to be questioned is a sure characteristic of authoritarian power. Authority deserves to be questioned. We owe it to those in authority to keep them on their toes. Genuine authority wants to be questioned, because only through continual respectful questioning can those in power overcome the temptation of thinking that they have all the answers. No one does; life is too surprising for that.

The gazelle jumps,
and should her fawn crawl?
—FULFULDE

Flies' eggs hatch flies.
—CHINESE

A crab doesn't hatch a bird.
—GA, GOLD COAST

What can you expect
from a pig but a grunt?
—IRISH

According to John's gospel Jesus says: "I have come that they may have life, life in abundance" (10:10). Life creates ever new forms. Old structures support new life and growth, but then they harden and must be replaced. Every living organism and every ecosystem continually renews itself. A common sense animates and guides the whole. New growth knows when to spring up; old structures know when to let go. When the raspberries are ripe, they drop from the briars; when the milkweed seeds are ready, the pods split open to let the wind carry the little suns away. When the coyote mother becomes aware that her pups can now hunt for themselves, she wanders off and leaves the territory to the young. Only in human society does fearful clinging to power block common sense. Taoist sages were keenly aware of this. The more they attuned themselves to nature, the more they despised and ridiculed their society's aberrations from Common Sense. Jesus contrasts these aberrations of a death-bound world with a world alive by God's life-breath—the Holy Spirit.

If "Holy Spirit" were not a time-honored term, we would never call the experiential reality to which it refers by this name. When we speak of a spirit today, what first comes to mind is a ghost. And "holy"—as in "Holy Moly!"—no longer implies a sense of reverence and awe. If we had to come up with an expression for the harmony-creating life force that connects all with all and with the very source of life, "Common Sense" would be most appropriate and readily available. Each time we see "Holy Spirit" printed on a page or hear it said aloud, we might replace it with "Common Sense" to get the full impact.

Using the imagery of his Jewish tradition, Jesus calls his vision of a world in which harmony reigns "the kingdom of God." In our age, kings belong to the realm of fairy tales. Obedience to a supreme ruler is no longer a value that inspires us. A pyramid of authority with king and god—or even God—on top is a defunct model; today's emerging model is closer to what Gary Snyder calls "Earth Household." Here, authority works from within: the family spirit of Common Sense makes all work in harmony with all. The "kingdom" that Jesus envisages is a "God Household." He sees God not so much as our King, but as our Father; and the motherly Spirit (originally a feminine term) is an all-pervading sense of family, our Common Sense. In the God Household, the love of power yields to the power of love.

"The smaller the lizard, the greater its ambition to become a crocodile," they say in Ethiopia. It's hard to assess if this is true among reptiles, but it is certainly true among humans. The degree of power one wields determines one's place in the authority pyramid of a worldly kingdom. But the kingdom of Heaven has the authority structure of a household. Here, the mark of authority is service: "Let the greatest among you become as the least, and the leader as the one who serves" (Luke 22:26). In the God Household, those in authority must use their power to empower all who are under their authority. ✾

You can do without friends,
but not without neighbors.
—EGYPTIAN

No one is so rich
as to need no neighbor.
—HUNGARIAN

We are mice of the same hole:
If we don't meet going in,
we meet coming out.
—HAUSA, EAST

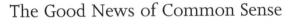

The Good News of Common Sense

The message of Jesus implies that inner rather than outer authority ought to guide us: The time has come; a common-sense world inspired by the power of love is at hand; let this turn your old outlook on life upside down; put your whole heart into living in this good newness! (See Mark 1:15.)

We can group the gospel parables quite naturally into five sets according to the way they relate to this central message.

1. Parables signaling the end of an unjust and exploitative world order.

2. Parables speaking of new life stirring, as in buds bursting, dough rising, and seed sprouting.

3. Parables alerting us to expect the unexpected.

4. Parables challenging us to seize the moment, to act as if everything depended entirely on us yet to trust in God and be patient.

5. Parables about a new order—an order of love—in answer to the perennial question that Piet Hein formulates as: "I want to know what this whole show is all about, before it's out." Wouldn't we all want to know? Jesus offers this common-sense answer: It's all about celebration; it all leads up to a great wedding feast.

1. The old order is collapsing.

As we set out to examine the parables in these different sets, let's start with the ones that tell us that we need not take the world as we find it or for what it pretends to be—it is not the real thing. It is a world out of tune with common sense. Jesus invites us to judge for ourselves. "A good tree brings forth good fruit." Right? Of course! "But a corrupt tree brings forth evil fruit" (Matthew 7:17), isn't that so? Of course it is. Well then, look at oppression, violence, exploitation. . . . Do you think the tree that bears such fruit is basically sound? Do you still think our society is basically healthy? What good do you expect from it? "What does one gather from brambles? A cluster of grapes? Or from thistles? Figs?" (Matthew 7:16). Unlikely as it is, most people expect that the thorns and thistles of a political establishment built on force will yield good fruit, if only we wait long enough. As to the religious establishment, "Can the blind lead the blind?" (Luke 6:39). If life were whitewater rafting, would you entrust yourself to a guide with no better qualifications than having studied books on the matter? To whom are you entrusting yourself in your "exploration into God"? Is the teaching you receive salted with the salt of common sense? "Salt is good, but when it loses its saltiness, with what will you season it?" (Mark 9:50) remains a question worth pondering.

The assessment Jesus makes of his own time makes me wonder how he would assess ours. The state of the world remains bad news. We may not yet know what to do about it, but common sense can tell us at least that a world order based on power and exploitation is not sustainable. "Even if you can't lay eggs, you can smell when one is rotten," a proverb from Serbia says.

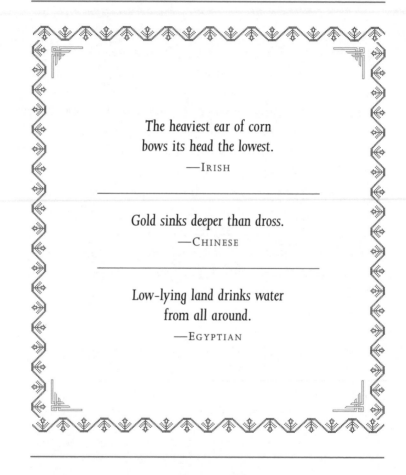

The heaviest ear of corn
bows its head the lowest.

—IRISH

Gold sinks deeper than dross.

—CHINESE

Low-lying land drinks water
from all around.

—EGYPTIAN

"Can't you tell that there is a carcass nearby, when you see carrion birds gathering overhead?" (Matthew 24:28). "Something is rotten in the state of Denmark." Are you pretending not to be aware of it? "When you see a cloud rising in the west, you say at once, 'A shower is coming'; and so it happens. And when you see the south wind blowing, you say, 'There will be scorching heat'; and it happens. You play-actors! You know how to interpret the appearance of earth and sky, but why do you not know how to interpret the present time?" (Luke 12:54–56). The answer to this question is already implied by the phrase "You play-actors!"—usually left in its Greek form, "hypocrites!" We must choose: either act the part that a sick society assigns to us, or stand up for common sense.

2. A new life is stirring.

When we grow alert to the signs of the times, we see positive signs, too: a new season is stirring. "When cocoa ripe, him must burst," a Jamaican proverb says. In Palestine, it's not the cocoa bean but the bud on the fig tree that bursts open. "Look at the fig tree and all the trees; as soon as they bud forth, you see for yourselves and know that summer is near" (Luke 21:29–30). "Can't you see for yourselves?" Jesus asks. The bad news is inseparable from the Good News. "A woman in labor has pain, for her hour has come, but when she has born the child, she no longer remembers her distress for joy" (John 16:21). Can't you see this happening all around you?

Common sense knows: What is truly new does not make its entrance with pomp and fanfare; it is small, quiet, and hidden. Still, it has the power to transform, "like leaven which a woman took and hid in three measures of meal, till it was all leavened" (Luke 13:21). Three measures of flour make a huge quantity of dough, yet the leaven is completely hidden in it. Seed, too, is hidden in the ground—"like a grain of mustard seed, which, when sown upon the ground, is the smallest of all seeds on earth; yet, when it is sown it grows up and becomes the greatest of all shrubs" (Mark 4:31–32).

New growth is vulnerable: much seed goes to waste in the sowing. "A sower went out to sow his seed; and as he sowed, some fell along the path, and was trodden under foot, and the birds of the air devoured it. And some fell on the rock; and as it grew up, it withered away, because it had no moisture. And some fell among thorns; and the thorns grew with it and choked it" (Luke 8:5–8). And yet, "Some fell into good soil and grew, and yielded a hundredfold"—amply making up for all the losses. Nor should we pull up the weeds that seem to choke the wheat, "lest in gathering the weeds you root up the wheat along with them. Let both grow together until the harvest" (Matthew 13:29–30). Why do we so quickly grow impatient? The seed is growing. The bread is rising. All we need is patience.

Our common sense, if we'd but use it, is in tune with the patience of nature, "as if a man should scatter seed upon the ground, and should sleep and rise night and day, and the seed should sprout and grow, he knows not how. The earth produces of itself, first the blade, then the ear, then the full grain in the ear. But when the grain is ripe, at once he puts in the sickle, because the harvest has come" (Mark 4:26–29). "Indolence is often taken for patience," says a French proverb. But the truly patient are anything but indolent: they know

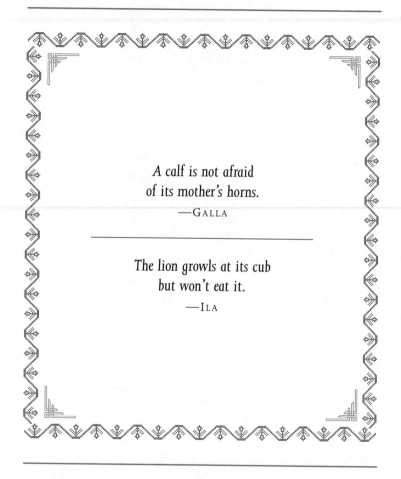

A calf is not afraid
of its mother's horns.
—GALLA

The lion growls at its cub
but won't eat it.
—ILA

when to act. Wide-awake to the right moment for the harvest, the reaper in Jesus' parable puts in the sickle "at once." Common sense gives us both patience to wait and alertness to strike while the iron is hot.

3. Now is the moment.

Another set of parables gives us flash images to sharpen our sense for the decisive moment. Someone's sudden death, a lightning flash, a burglary: challenges to expect the unexpected. "The land of a rich man brought forth plentifully; and he thought to himself, 'What shall I do, for I have nowhere to store my crops?' And he said, 'I will do this: I will pull down my barns and build larger ones; and there I will store all my grain and my goods. And I will say to my soul, Soul, you have ample goods laid up for many years; take your ease, eat, drink, enjoy yourself.'" The broad flow of this narrative makes the ending sound all the more sudden: "Fool! This very night your life will be demanded back from you" (Luke 12:16–20). "Death keeps no calendar," as the English proverb says. Neither does a burglar make an appointment. "If the householder had known at what hour the thief was coming" (Luke 12:39), he would have watched. Watch out! Can you foretell the moment when lightning will strike? Or, in the colorful language of a proverb from the southern United States, "Mule don't kick according to no rule."

In a time of momentous change, we must be awake and alert. We must watch out for sudden opportunity and, when it pops up, go after it. We must be ready at a moment's notice to let go of the old and invest everything we have in the new order.

Expecting nothing, a plowman plods along. With a clank, his plowshare hits hidden treasure. What would you do? He doesn't think twice. "In his joy he goes and sells all that he has and buys that field" (Matthew 13:44). Another—a merchant in search of fine pearls—is already on the alert. He knows a priceless pearl at first sight—and he goes for broke (Matthew 13:45–46). Common sense is as daring as it is patient. "Nothing wagered, nothing won."

4. Trust in God, yet act as if everything depended entirely on you alone.

In a particularly colorful series of parables, the main characters are, above all, enterprising. Some industrious servants—first-century venture capitalists—double the money their master entrusted to them. With great determination, a man makes a nuisance of himself by coaxing his friend out of bed in the middle of the night and gets what he needs. An obstinate old woman pesters a judge so relentlessly that he promises a just sentence on her behalf even though he is corrupt to the bone. A manager who has embezzled money and is about to lose his job feathers his bed for an early retirement by quickly embezzling a good deal more. These are not edifying stories featuring models to be imitated, but jokes that make a point: Doesn't common sense tell you that one has to use one's wits to get ahead in life? You know this? Why then don't you put some effort into making this a better world, a world run by common sense? Why don't you start now? As the Bantu say, "If you want to sweep the hut, why do you sit on the broom?"

One who rides in a litter doesn't realize
how far it is to town.

—HAUSA

Those who wear pearls do not know how often
the shark bites the diver.

—ETHIOPIA

Mr. Fullbelly doesn't know Mr. Hollowbelly.

—GERMAN

One eats the roast; the other licks the spit.

—HUNGARIAN

One who hasn't carried your burden
knows not its weight.

—HAYA, EAST AFRICA

And yet, in our spiritual practice, the supreme goal of all effort is to make no effort. This, too, common sense teaches us—the sense we have in common with the "birds of the air" and the wildflowers. "Consider the ravens: they neither sow nor reap, they have neither storehouse nor barn, and yet God feeds them. . . . Consider the lilies how they grow; they neither toil nor spin; yet I tell you, not even Solomon in all his glory was arrayed like one of these" (Luke 12:24–27). In the midst of acting as if the outcome depended entirely on us, we can live carefree lives because God cares.

How do we know that God cares? We know that God cares because we care. This answer is the most staggering implication of Jesus' parables: To follow the guidance of common sense is to share the mind of God. Decades before the parables were written down, Paul put his finger on this crucial point. "The Spirit reaches the depth of everything, even the depth of God" (1 Corinthians 2:10). In the parables, Jesus presupposes precisely this. He often speaks of the unique intimacy and mutual understanding between a father and a son. Is not this deep understanding implied when we call God "Our Father"?

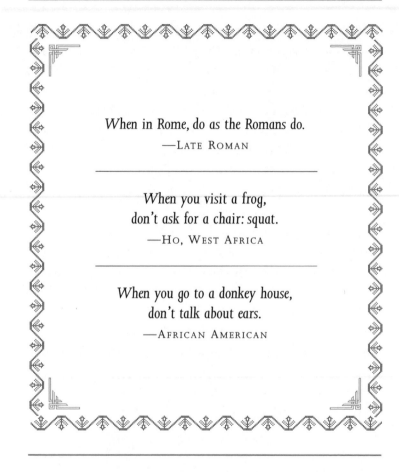

When in Rome, do as the Romans do.

—LATE ROMAN

When you visit a frog,
don't ask for a chair: squat.

—HO, WEST AFRICA

When you go to a donkey house,
don't talk about ears.

—AFRICAN AMERICAN

It may seem an outrageous claim that we humans share the mind of God, and yet in some situations most of us spontaneously act on this conviction. For example, when a theologian claims that God predestines some creatures to eternal suffering or excludes from heaven children who died before they were baptized, common sense revolts. We are convinced that this cannot be so. On what could our reaction be based if not on a deep-seated conviction that we can somehow know the mind of God—at least in matters that are vital for us humans?

The finest parables of Jesus evoke strong common-sense attitudes and trigger the insight that God shares these attitudes. "What father among you, if his son asks for a fish, will instead of a fish give him a serpent; or if he asks for an egg, will give him a scorpion?" (Luke 11:11–12). In Matthew's gospel, Jesus asks, "Who among you, if his son asks for bread, will give him a stone? If you then . . . know how to give good gifts to your children, how much more will your Father who is in heaven give good things to those who ask him?" (7:9–11). Jesus stretches the notion of commonness so far that common sense allows us to sense even God's sentiments. The pattern "If you

There is no elbow that bends outwards.
—CHINESE

You cannot coax the morning glory
to climb the wrong way
round the corn stalk.
—AFRICAN AMERICAN

You can lead the horse to the water,
but you can't make it drink.
—ENGLISH

. . . then all the more, God" is the basis for many parables.

The best known of all Jesus' parables is based on this pattern. We call it the Parable of the Prodigal Son, but it is really about the feelings of a prodigal father. We must not project today's stereotype of a father on Jesus' notion of God. The father in this story stands for God, but he acts every bit like a Jewish mother. He sees his wayward son returning from afar (obviously, he has been watching and waiting at the window); he smothers the son's self-accusations in hugs and kisses; he quickly notices the boy's dirty clothes and makes him change into clean ones; he cooks up a storm and prepares a feast. (We will come back to that feast.) When the older, law-abiding son objects to all this festivity, the father insists: "We do have to make merry and celebrate, for your brother was lost and is found"(Luke 15:32).

If we rejoice when a wayward child returns home, how much more does God rejoice? There are parallels to this in other parables: the joy of a shepherd over a lost-and-found sheep (Luke 15:4–7); the joy of a woman who turns the whole house upside down until she finds the coin she had lost

If you are not going
to eat your porridge,
stop stirring it.
—HAUSA

If you ferry at all,
ferry right over.
—CHINESE

(Luke 15:8–10). Who doesn't know how precious and important something becomes the moment we lose it—or are merely afraid to lose it? Those of us who spend more on repair bills than our old watch is worth will feel deeply with the gardener who pleads with the owner to give an obviously worthless fig tree just one more chance (Luke 13:6–9). Even to such a "silly" sentiment, Jesus applies the pattern, "If you . . . how much more, God." What makes this argument so convincing is that it is based on common sense. When we let these sayings of Jesus sink in, we discover how profound they are—and at the same time how outrageous.

The parables are profound because it is common sense that makes them tick, and common sense—like the *Tao* and the *Logos*—is the deepest undercurrent of the cosmic flow. They are outrageous because they challenge time-honored conventions: for instance, the notion that we must merit what we receive—wages must be based on service rendered. In one parable, the day laborers are all paid a day's wages regardless of whether they have sweated all day or were hired only an hour before day's end. By conventional standards, this is

Nobody's family can hang up the sign,
"Nothing the matter here."
—CHINESE

There are no cattle without a dung heap.
—CHUANA

Every family has a skeleton in the closet.
—AMERICAN

Every cabin has its mosquito.
—AFRICAN AMERICAN

Chicken says: "If you scratch too hard,
you come upon the bones of your mother."
—AFRICAN JABO

unfair, but common sense tells us otherwise. How could they have worked earlier if no one hired them? And how could they and their families eat that evening unless they received a day's wages? Admittedly, even in the God Household there is a realm where merit has its proper place. It does matter what we do, or fail to do, with our talents. Yet, isn't our very existence pure gift to begin with? Ultimately, all is grace.

5. A new order: Not drudgery, but celebration.

What makes a parable tick is the ticking of a time bomb that goes off the moment we get the point. Common sense blows conventional notions to bits.

Even the notion of "serving God" is exploded. No matter how much we are accustomed to thinking of our relationship to God as that of servants to a lord and king, Jesus uses the leverage of common sense to lift us out of that rut. Isn't the King of Heaven your Father? "'What do you think, Simon? From whom do the kings of the world take tribute or taxes? From their children or from strangers?' and when he said, 'From strangers,' Jesus replied, 'Then the children are exempt'"(Matthew

Need breaks laws.
—DUTCH

Law makes law-breakers.
—BANTU

The law is a spider's web:
Big flies break through,
but the little ones get caught.
—HUNGARIAN

17:25–26). You are princes and princesses: You are tax exempt!

Once we realize this, we no longer drudge along in servitude but freely and joyfully offer our gifts to God. "The spirit you received is not the spirit of slaves, bringing fear into your lives, but the spirit of sonship in which we call out, 'Abba, Father!'" (Romans 8:15). Such common-sense teaching is heady wine. Will anyone put new wine like this into old wine skins? "If one does, the wine will burst the skins, and the wine is lost, and so are the skins"(Mark 2:22).

From early on, however, the followers of Jesus have tried to do just this: tried to contain the new spirit within the old forms. The result is compromise—patchwork. "No one sews a piece of un-shrunk cloth on an old garment; if he does, the patch tears away from it, the new from the old, and a worse tear is made (Mark 2:21). That's common sense. Yet, for almost two millennia now, church institutions have suffered rift after rift because of precisely such patchwork.

One handy example is fasting as a prescribed religious observance. Voluntary fasting can be a healthy practice. There are many good reasons for fasting, but earning God's favor thereby is not one of them. God's love—like a mother's—need not be earned, only celebrated, Jesus held. He did not fast; in fact, they called him "a glutton and a drunkard" (Matthew 11:19). His favorite image for life in fullness was a great feast, a royal wedding feast, to which everyone—high and low, rich and poor—was invited. "Can you make wedding guests fast?" (Luke 5:34), he asked. He did not want his followers bound by religious observances but freed for a great celebration. Soon, however, they reinstituted fasting on the grounds that Jesus, the bridegroom, was "taken away from them" (Matthew 9:15), in spite of the fact that, in the same gospel, he was quoted as saying, "I am with you all the days until the end of time"(28:20). In this, as in many other points, conventional religious practice won out over the spirit of Jesus. And yet, the same religious institutions that are to blame for this shift of focus deserve our thanks for having preserved for us the common-sense sayings of Jesus. Now, as then, these sayings challenge prevailing practices.

One of Jesus' most amusing parables addresses the tension between ascetic religious observance and celebration in the Spirit. We might call it the Parable of the House Left Standing

Empty (Matthew 12:43–45). Here the classical pattern of Jesus' parable telling has not been preserved, but we can easily restore it.

Step one, the opening question: Don't you know what happens to a house when you sweep it and decorate it and then let it stand empty? Think of a holiday cabin on the shore or in the woods. Say it came to you as an inheritance. You are thrilled; you dream already of parties you will have there and you spend every spare hour fixing it up. Soon it looks spic-and-span. But just when all is ready, your children lose interest; other plans interfere, weekend after weekend. What do you expect that place to look like when you finally return? Moldy, mildewed, full of mice and squirrels, bugs and spiders.

This is already step two, the common-sense answer to the opening question. We have merely updated the gospel imagery and replaced evil spirits with rodents and insects. A place left standing empty—and empty is the operative word here—will be worse in the end than before you put so much effort into fixing it up. Common sense tells us this.

Hence, step three, the implied question: Why then do you put so much effort into inner "housecleaning," without ever

'Tis a good word
that can better a good silence.
—DUTCH

Words are silver, silence is gold.
—GERMAN

The stars make no noise.
—IRISH

getting around to having that party for which you have uncluttered and cleaned and adorned your heart? Once again, the joke is on us, because we are reminded of a truth we know deep down, but fail to act upon: the goal of asceticism is celebration—and not later, either, but here and now. The very housecleaning ought to be done in the spirit of a party.

Throughout the ages and in our own time, countless followers of Jesus have done this and are still doing it. They make ascetical practice come aglow from within. In the midst of misery and in spite of all adversity they suffer for their convictions, they celebrate the great wedding feast. Didn't we come across this image before in our exploration of common sense? Yes, we did—when we found common sense alive in the hum and buzz of a meadow. Here, at the level of human society, we must lose nothing of what we witnessed there among plants and animals, but we must add the specifically human elements of freedom and responsibility. To build a common-sense society that is in tune with the great cosmic wedding feast—that's what "this whole show is all about," and this fact is good news indeed. ✺

Telling the truth is not a sin,
but it causes inconvenience.

—MEXICAN

A child, a drunkard,
and a fool tell the truth.

—HUNGARIAN

Seeing is believing,
but feeling is God's own truth.

—IRISH

Truth has all the benefits
of sham without the disadvantages.

—DUTCH

Obstacles to Common Sense

J esus, if he came today, might look bewildered at what has become of the movement he started. Would he recognize it at all? Would he think it has much to do with the message he preached? I think he would feel more at home in a twelve-step meeting than in most Christian churches, let alone in the Vatican. But this should not surprise us. Other spiritual masters of the past would be no better off. Lao Tsu would be at a loss searching for vital signs of the *Tao* in a Taoist temple and any philosophy department would make Heraclitus feel like the proverbial fish out of water. Yet, all three of these great teachers still have fervent followers today. As for Jesus, there are still—within the churches and without—countless men and women who are aglow with his spirit because they have understood his message. They live by common sense—in

Children talk with God.
—CHUANA

*A child who asks questions
isn't stupid.*
—EWE

A lovely child has many names.
—HUNGARIAN

Honor a child and it will honor you.
—ILA

Children are the wisdom of the nation.
—JABO

more traditional terms, they are "led by the Spirit of God" (Romans 8:14).

Twelve-step programs rely on no other authority than common sense. Jesus would recognize his spirit alive and active today as soon as he walked into a twelve-step meeting. This should not surprise us, since the founders of Alcoholics Anonymous were fervent Christians. And there is an even deeper connection between sobriety and common sense. Don't we call people who use common sense "sober minded"? What then is the addiction that makes most of us, again and again, fall off the wagon of common sense? It must be an enormously strong addiction to draw so many into its spell.

What is it that attracts us with such power? For many years I was searching for an answer to this question. What is the desire that draws us away from common sense? Gradually, the answer dawned on me: It is our longing to belong. But does not this deep desire in the human heart aim precisely at that all-embracing communion from which common sense springs? Isn't our homesickness a desire for the cosmic household of which common sense is the family spirit? Indeed it is.

But we fail to go all the way. We settle too soon, settle for less, before we reach our true home.

This is true for every addiction. Our goal is something good that attracts us. The higher the good, the stronger the attraction. The stronger also the addiction if we do not go on until we reach the goal, but halfway there settle for less and cling to that. Thus, one may seek for some high value—contentment, peace of mind, fellowship—find a little bit of it in the bar at the corner, and get no further than a drunken binge and a hangover. Likewise, we may find our longing to belong partly satisfied by a community that falls far short of being all-embracing, cling to this partial fulfillment of our desire, and end up with a common narrow-mindedness that is anything but common sense. "Ra! Ra! Ra! My country—or my university, my union, my church—right or wrong!"

Let's not be too hard on ourselves. Settling for less is a perennial temptation, and so is its opposite: restless exploring. In each of us there is the settler and the explorer. Both are driven by fear. The settler fears change; the explorer fears boredom. In our explorer mode, we are so enamored with the seeking that we fear nothing so much as finding, for this would bring the search for our heart's desire to an end. In our settler mode, in contrast, we are so eager to find that we cut the search short.

But we are all pilgrims. In the pilgrim, explorer and settler are united. Pilgrims have a double courage: the explorers' courage to go beyond the familiar and the settlers' courage to be content with it. On a pilgrimage, each step is the goal, yet each goal may turn out to be just a step on the road that leads on—we must not cling to it.

Clinging is our problem as pilgrims through life. And clinging springs from fear. It is basically a healthy reflex. Newborn babies, when frightened, reach up with arms and legs in an effort to cling to their mothers—an instinct that may go back to an age when our mothers were still leaping from branch to branch and we'd better hang on when danger threatened. We retain this instinct for our entire lives. When fear takes hold of us, we grasp and cling, mentally no less than bodily. What is new always seems threatening at first. If we want to grow, expand, and go forward into new territory, we must learn to let go of the old.

No goat can butt alone.

—SWISS

A single bracelet doesn't jingle.

—FULFULDE

One key doesn't rattle.

—CHINESE

One somebody can't quarrel.

—AFRICAN AMERICAN

For most of us, the communion we have with our mothers before we are born is perfect. Yet we must let go of it and be on our own before we can find communion on a new level. Whenever we move forward to a new and wider community, it is like another birth—often not less difficult and painful. What is so frightening is that we must step out, speak up, and go it alone. To push beyond the mental horizon of those with whom we felt at home and to push on towards ever wider horizons takes great courage. Fear is the great obstacle to us— fear of losing our friends, of being ridiculed, of being ostracized, of standing alone. Unless we can overcome our fear, we will cling to what is at hand and get addicted to it. In every society the pressure to conform is powerful. Many of us are cowards when it comes to going it alone.

Imagine a twelve-step program for Cowards Anonymous, meetings in which members would support one another in standing up fearlessly for common sense. Instead, we are more like the citizens in Hans Christian Andersen's story "The Emperor's New Suit." All it took was two swindlers who claimed to weave garments for the king that would be invisible

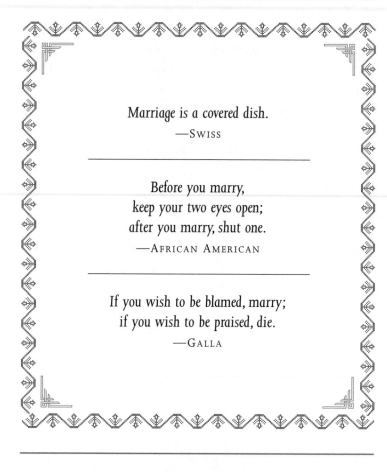

Marriage is a covered dish.
—SWISS

Before you marry,
keep your two eyes open;
after you marry, shut one.
—AFRICAN AMERICAN

If you wish to be blamed, marry;
if you wish to be praised, die.
—GALLA

to anyone unfit for office or stupid beyond words. Who would admit to this? From the emperor on down, everyone claimed to see what wasn't there and admired the beautiful clothes. One supported the other, as the whole population silently conspired to maintain the lie, and the emperor in his make-believe new suit paraded down the street stark naked. "But he has nothing on at all!" a little child called out at last, breaking the spell. "Children and fools speak the truth," a proverb declares. Why shouldn't they? They have nothing invested in the status quo. Unless we "become like little children" (Matthew 18:3), we will find the obstacles to common sense insurmountable. Only common sense can make you free. 🏵

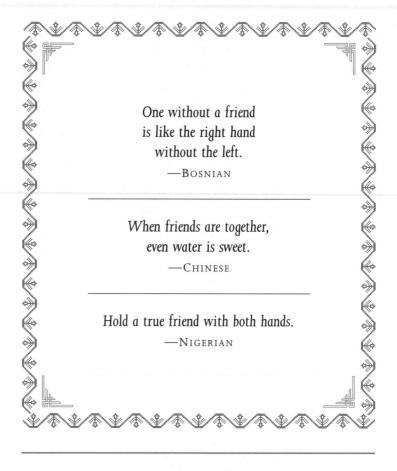

One without a friend
is like the right hand
without the left.
—BOSNIAN

When friends are together,
even water is sweet.
—CHINESE

Hold a true friend with both hands.
—NIGERIAN

Cultivating Common Sense

Think of your favorite piece of music. Remember what it feels like when you hear that piece. Something deep within you starts resonating. Maybe there comes a moment when it becomes "music heard so deeply that it isn't heard at all, but you are the music while the music lasts" (as T. S. Eliot put it in *The Four Quartets*). Here you are attuning yourself to music through your sense of hearing; through common sense, you can attune yourself in a similar way to the harmony of the cosmos. Common sense is a *sense*—just like hearing, tasting, or smelling—and we can cultivate it just as we cultivate our other senses. There are people who have so refined their sense of taste that they can tell in what soil the grapes for a certain wine were grown. Through that sense we call "common," you can "taste"—in everything you experience—the soil in which all of us are rooted. Every child is born with this sense. It is our birthright as humans. We need only cultivate it.

Cultivating common sense is a lifelong task. Here I will point out three aspects of the task: attuning ourselves to nature, developing a support system, and learning to question authority. But to cultivate common sense is not only a task— it is a lifelong joy. Nothing gives you more joy than when your heart grows wider and wider and your sense of belonging to the universe grows deeper and deeper. It is a healing process. Anyone can tell that our society must be sick by looking at what we are doing to nature: We make nature sick. That's the bad news. The good news is that we can tap into the living spring of still healthy nature and so heal ourselves and society again. By failing to use common sense, we humans have become cosmic outlaws. Our most urgent task is to recover our kinship with nature.

To expose ourselves to nature, it is not necessary to travel to the Grand Canyon or to some Pacific island. What we must change is not our geographic location but our inner attitude. With dulled hearts, we will merely bring noise and pollution to the most pristine environment; yet to alert inner eyes, trees in a pitiful city park or merely the weeds on the empty lots of slums can speak of patience, tenacity, and much that goes beyond words. Sparrows will come to you almost anywhere if you throw them a few breadcrumbs; if you open your heart to these little gray and brown sisters and brothers, they will tell you that you are not alone. Even the caged animals in a zoo, painful as it is to encounter them there, will speak to us if we learn to listen.

As a young man, I wandered one evening into a small zoo, mostly for children, at the southeast corner of Central Park in New York City. It must have been nearly closing time, because there were no other people around and even the animals seemed to be asleep in the recesses behind their cages. In one cage, however, an ancient gorilla was squatting. His forehead was deeply furrowed. Our eyes met. One look, and I stood under his spell. Our silent, motionless interview may have lasted an hour or more. I was too young then to fully appreciate the wisdom he unlocked for me. Now that I am old, I remember this encounter almost every day. Our communication

*A single general's fame
is made of ten thousand corpses.*

—CHINESE

No one becomes a good doctor
before filling a churchyard.

—SWEDISH

continues, and I think gratefully of this simian elder as one of my great teachers.

Televised nature programs can be great experiences, too. They can alert us to our kinship with all life, but they are usually fast paced and scientific rather than poetic in their approach. We need to cultivate a poetic, meditative openness to nature. Photographs from a nature calendar may help us learn a deep and quiet looking with the eyes of our heart. This practice attunes us to the cosmic current that pulsates in the depths of every mountain and forest, of the Milky Way, and of the humblest head of cabbage. Our most elevated thoughts and our grandest endeavors will be healthy only inasmuch as we are connected to the life we have in common with that cabbage and with all the rest of the cosmos.

The more exposure to nature makes us sense that we belong to a cosmic family, the more we are likely to feel ill at ease in mainstream society. We look at the forest and see it as a community to which we belong; most people look at the same woods as a commodity that belongs to us. To find at least a few people with whom we can communicate on a common-sense

Don't loose the falcon
'til you see the hare.
—CHINESE

Don't throw the old bucket away
'til you know that
the new one holds water.
—SWEDISH

See the candle light
before you blow out the match.
—AFRICAN AMERICAN

level will be essential for our spiritual survival. If we are lucky, likeminded friends will strengthen us in taking a common-sense stand. Some of our strongest support may come from people we never meet in person—authors of books, commentators on public radio and television, people we meet via the Internet. We do need the support of others, because we can easily feel isolated in questioning prevailing opinions and policies.

Support does not always mean agreement. Friends also support us by challenging our opinions on the ground of common sense. We must learn to listen not only to the voice of common sense as we hear it, but to the voices of others who hear and interpret it differently. Only this twofold listening can save us from self-deception. How well I am listening with the ear of my heart can best be tested by finding out how well I am listening with the ears of my head. The best test for common sense is common deliberation. Only by producing consensus will common sense be truly common. There is no shortcut to consensus, but even a long and tedious road to it will be worth the effort. Decision by majority vote is to consensus what marching in parade step is to waltzing. Dancers must listen to the same music; this is why we must question whether it is the same authority we obey.

I was twelve when Hitler invaded Austria, and my teens were overshadowed by the swastika. This taught me early in life to question authority, to ask, "Who says so?" It can still be a helpful habit to ask the question while you listen to the evening news. "Who says so?" In whose interest is it to tell us a particular piece of news in these words and with this perspective? Friends say to me, "If we had lived then, we too would have questioned authority." Well, can you be sure you would have done it then unless you are questioning authority now? There is no time or place, no situation, in which we can afford to stop questioning to what extent we are in tune with common sense. Questioning basic assumptions is as essential to our safety as checking the launching pad of a rocket is for the safety of astronauts.

At any point in history, we are all like the crew of a spaceship at countdown. In times like our own, the countdown seems even more clearly audible. We are taking off for an unimaginable future. Everything is changing. Common sense had been steering the universe from change to change for vast stretches of time, before we humans ever arrived. We cannot stop change. But we can cultivate common sense so that the changes for which we and our society are responsible will be in tune with the creative force of the universe—call it the *Tao*, the *Logos*, or Dante's "Love that moves the sun and all the stars."